WELCOME TO

Whether you are coming as an individual, part of a group, or as a whole church following our Sunday resources, we are really pleased to be with you on this Advent journey.

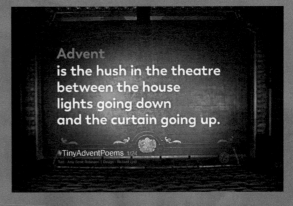

The #TinyAdventPoems by Amy Scott Robinson capture so vividly the heart of *Worship in the Waiting*. Advent is a unique invitation to anticipate, to live with holy, awe-filled expectancy as we approach the celebration of Christmas. It offers us a period of preparation, both physically and spiritually, for the gift that is about to be born.

Waiting in the Bible

Hebrews 11 lists a host of Bible characters who lived by faith, waiting for the fulfilment of God's promises to them. Even Jesus himself waited 30 years before beginning his earthly ministry. God, according to Peter, "is not slow in keeping his promise, as some understand slowness. Instead he is patient with you" (2 Pet 3:9). The Bible invites us to enter into God's patient, unhurried pace, and see ourselves transformed into more Christ-like people in the process.

Waiting today

We wrote this material in 2020, when Covid-19 and lockdown made "waiting" highly relevant. We feel that these themes will resonate for Advent 2020 and for many years to come. To help you engage in varied ways we have included things like reflection questions with space to scribble your responses, ideas for creative interaction, and practical steps to work out the teaching in everyday life.

How the weeks work

There is a reflection for each weekday of Advent. We think it is realistic that weekends might be busy, or they might be a good time to catch up on a day you missed during the week.

Our series also includes an "intro week" before the first week of Advent, so check the calendar for when to start these devotionals. After the 4th week of Advent we have left the reflections un-numbered, to allow you to read the Christmas Day reflection on whatever day it falls.

If your church is following our Sunday material, you should find that the weekly reflections unpack and complement this. If you want to engage as a small group, you can easily adapt the questions and responses to fit group discussion.

#TinyAdventPoems

We began this introduction quoting one of Amy's poems, which were visually presented so brilliantly by Richard Lyall in 2019 and were enthusiastically received on social media. We will post them daily through Advent on Twitter, Facebook and Instagram, so do share and use them as you like (search #TinyAdventPoems or visit engageworship.org/TinyAdventPoems).

Advent:
the table is set,
the balloons blown up,
bunting hung.
We jump at each crunch
of footstep on gravel
in the driveway.

#TinyAdventPoems 15/24
Text - Amy Scott Robinson | Design - Richard Lyall

Waiting for a King

INTRO WEEK

0.1 - AN ADVENT WAITING JOURNEY
"I wait for the Lord, my whole being waits."
(Psalm 130:5)

Read: Psalm 130

"Advent" means "coming". When we believe that something is coming, we live in an in-between state. When friends or family are about to arrive at our home for a celebration we might run around tidying up, glancing at the clock or out the window. We are not yet experiencing the fullness of our guests' presence, and at the same time we act in expectation of their appearance. When we're waiting for Christmas dinner to be served we may experience boredom, hunger, impatience, and at the same time we can anticipate the good meal we're about to enjoy. When children know that there are gifts coming they might nag their parents, or try to sneak a peek under the wrapping paper, and at the same time they are learning patience (whether they like it or not!).

How have you approached Advent in the past? Has it centred around a chocolate calendar, or perhaps the lighting of special candles? Or maybe it has got trampled under the rush to buy gifts, organise parties and finish work ready for some time off?

Reflect: Write down some of your previous experiences of Advent below:

What if, this year, you decided to dedicate Advent to *waiting*? What would it look like to not rush ahead but to pause, to anticipate, to be expectant? The psalmist wrote about waiting for God with their "whole being". They looked expectantly for God to come and restore them: "I wait for the Lord, more than watchmen wait for the morning" (130:6).

Let's not forget that this is the psalm which begins: "Out of the depths I cry to you, Lord." This waiting is a result of struggle and hardship. The writer cries out to God for mercy, trusting in God's faithfulness when all around them is crumbling.

We are writing this devotional in the middle of the 2020 Covid-19 crisis and global lockdown. We can't know when you are reading it, but it is hard to believe that we won't all look back on that time as an unprecedented period of waiting. As we write, nobody knows when the lockdown will end. No one can be sure of the full extent of the damage that will be done to families, economies and communities. We have no choice but to wait. But we have every choice about what *kind* of waiting we engage in.

Some waiting is anxious and impatient. It frets and worries, trying to hurry things along or taking out its insecurities on other people. But there is another kind of waiting - a godly waiting, where with the psalmist we choose to "put our hope in the Lord" (130:7). During this season we are going to explore aspects of what it means to worship God in the waiting.

Pray: Make this prayer your own:

Loving God, teach me to wait for you.
To wait with my whole being
- physically, soulfully, spiritually.
Teach me patience, teach me longing,
teach me to pray "Come, Lord Jesus".
Amen.

0.2 - A KING DISGUISED

"The King will reply... 'whatever you did for one of the least of these... you did for me.'"
(Matthew 25:40)

Read: Matthew 25:31-46

Some stories are so good they deserve being retold over and over again. A rich ruler hiding among the common people is one of those stories. In literature you have Mark Twain's *The Prince and The Pauper*, at the cinema we've seen Queen Amidala disguised as her maidservant in *Star Wars I: The Phantom Menace*, or if you're more into chickflicks you might know *The Prince and Me*. Similar real-life tales are told in the reality television show *The Secret Millionaire*, where wealthy people go incognito into impoverished communities to experience their full suffering, before revealing who they are and agreeing to give money away.

We are fascinated by this juxtaposition of a rich and powerful person experiencing the poor and mundane existence of the vast majority of humanity. How will they take to having to do their own cleaning? How will they experience a simple, home cooked meal? Will they learn something about themselves? Will they perhaps be able to love people so very different from them?

The way these stories are told, there's always a big "reveal" towards the end. Somehow the ordinary people discover that their friend / servant / lover is not exactly what they seem - the disguise is lost in favour of gold, jewels and fresh haircuts, leaving those around them shocked and awed.

Perhaps the true source of this often-told story lies in that of King Jesus. The long-expected ruler, the true heir of David's eternal throne, the one prophesied by Daniel, Isaiah and Jeremiah, comes not to Herod's palace as the Magi expect, but is laid into a manger in the small town of Bethlehem. The one who is in very nature God takes the form of a servant and is made human (Phil 2). He eats with the outcasts, spends time with the rejected and refuses to play the games of the rich and powerful around him.

As we will see tomorrow, hiding in plain sight among the poor has not diminished Jesus' kingly glory. But still, today, he continues to disguise himself as a pauper. In our passage we see him described to us as a king / judge holding court. And the judgments handed out are not based on the moral codes that Christians so often hold dear. There are no mentions of drinking, sexual immorality, telling lies or tithing. The King does not bring up heartfelt commitments made in sung worship, but seems to rather look for a different form of devotion. One that sees the King in the face of every poor and starving person, every hospital patient and every prisoner.

These fifteen verses are not a full theology of salvation, but rather act as a corrective for us. If the Pharisees and priests missed the King walking among them in the form of Jesus from Nazareth, what am I missing as I walk past the beggar outside the coffee shop? Jesus "... did not consider equality with God something to be grasped..." (Phil 2:6) and yet we so often scrabble and grasp for a rung higher up in the hierarchy of society.

I have a Gaelic rune of hospitality on my kitchen wall, and it acts as something of a summary of the passage of the Sheep and the Goats, correcting my vision as I live my life. I offer it here for reflection:

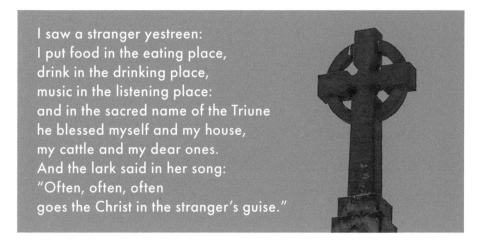

I saw a stranger yestreen:
I put food in the eating place,
drink in the drinking place,
music in the listening place:
and in the sacred name of the Triune
he blessed myself and my house,
my cattle and my dear ones.
And the lark said in her song:
"Often, often, often
goes the Christ in the stranger's guise."

Pray: Offer all your emotions coming out of today's reading to God. He will soothe fears, forgive shame, share joy and comfort sadness.

0.3 - THE KING'S TRUE COLOURS

"His face was like the sun shining in all its brilliance. When I saw him, I fell at his feet."
(Revelation 1:16-17)

Read: Revelation 1:12-18

Yesterday we considered the juxtaposition of Jesus, the King of Kings, taking on flesh and appearing as a poor man from Nazareth. The disciples were familiar with Jesus in this guise: Jesus, Son of Joseph, the manual labourer, was the man they knew and loved. Assuming that the John who wrote Revelation was "the disciple Jesus loved" (as he so beautifully calls himself in his gospel), the vision in today's passage must have been quite a shock. Yet, somehow this majestic Son of Man is recognised.

Jesus had, of course, revealed his true colours at least once before to his closest friends. In Luke 9 we read of Jesus taking Peter, James and John on a prayer retreat up a mountain. "As [Jesus] was praying, the appearance of his face changed and his clothes became as bright as a flash of lightning" (9:29). A flash of lightning is probably the brightest thing anyone had ever seen, then and now.

Mark telling the story, describes Jesus clothing as "...dazzling white, whiter than anyone in the world could bleach them" (Mark 9:3), whereas Matthew tells us that Jesus' "...face shone like the sun, and his clothes became as white as the light" (Matt 17:2). On Peter's state of mind at seeing this vision, Mark gives us this understated analysis: "He did not know what to say, they were so frightened" (v 6).

Although the disciples must have thought Jesus special (or they would not have followed him in the first place), to them, at the time, he was just a man. Someone with a similar hairstyle to them; who needed to wash, just like they did; who had favourite meals he looked forward to, just like they did. And then suddenly, they saw his true colours, his full identity as glorious and eternal. I think "frightened" would be the mildest adjective to describe how I would feel!

It is human to struggle to keep things in tension. We often fall into the ditch of considering God to be approachable and friendly, or holy and majestic. But he is both. Our King Jesus is both.

Create: Spend some time with John's vision of Jesus. If you enjoy drawing, perhaps follow John's description in Revelation 1:12-18 to sketch the main features. Or pick out important descriptive words and list them here, or form them into a poem. This will provide a form of meditation on the nature of King Jesus.

Pray: John "falls at [Jesus'] feet" (v 17) when faced with his glory. Could you assume something of that posture in prayer today? If possible, perhaps kneel or lay yourself out physically and see how that changes your approach to prayer and worship.

0.4 - PRACTICE RESURRECTION

"He raised Christ from the dead and seated him at his right hand... far above all rule and authority, power and dominion." (Ephesians 1:20-21)

Read: Ephesians 1:15-23

The words "king", "kingdoms" and "throne" are ones we associate with fairytales from childhood, or perhaps epic fantasy dramas made into excessively long movies or TV series. These words are found in dusty, old books; in fiction. The Advent invitation to wait for Jesus as "the coming King" can therefore feel as if it has little to do with reality.

However, try some other words from today's passage out for size: Rule. Authority. Power. Dominion. These are words not just found in old books, but can be found in today's newspaper, on the political blog you read, in the tweets of heads of state. We are aware of the authorities around us: the leaders we've elected as well as the subtler influence of big-business, tech companies and celebrity culture. Beyond that we are waking up to deeper, institutional biases and systemic prejudices which shape power-imbalances in our society.

In this complex system of many authorities and power-structures, what does it mean to wait for Jesus, our coming King?

The church in Ephesus knew about powers and authorities. Theirs was a city where Roman emperors were establishing and enforcing their rule, but it was also a centre of religious power. The cults and the deities they exalted were plentiful, and the power of magic was sought out and worshipped. To the Christians in this place, Paul writes that the battle is not against flesh and blood, but "against the powers of this dark world and against the spiritual forces of evil in the heavenly realms" (Eph 6:12).

Paul prays for this young church that their eyes would be opened to the "incomparably great power" (v 19) that they possess, through Christ. Do you think of yourself as having incomparably great power? If you don't, you might want to look at what else Paul prays for them in verse 18: that they would become aware of their "hope and inheritance".

Hope and inheritance are, by nature, to do with waiting. Yes, Jesus is the resurrected King, with every other power and authority below him. And yes, we share in this power. And yet, our hope is in a future when this is completely fulfilled; when we finally receive our full inheritance.

Paul's prayer is for the church to begin living out of the reality of these promises *now*. This is a reality "in the present age but also in the one to come" (v 21). The invitation is to step today into God's future for us, or (to use poet Wendell Berry's phrase) to "practice resurrection" in the here and now.

Reflect: Consider the situations around you or in your community where you feel powerless to bring change. What would it look like for you to "practice resurrection" today?

Pray: Speak out verses 18-23, exchanging all the "you's" for "I's". With eyes opened to your hope, your inheritance in Christ and your shared power with him, pray for change in the situations around you.

0.5 - A SUFFERING KING

Most coronations of new kings and queens are occasions of pomp and celebration. Monarchies have special gilded accessories that come out only for this event; ceremonial carriages get polished and throne rooms spruced up.

Of course, Jesus did not need a coronation: he is the eternal King, enthroned from before the beginning of time. And yet, the events leading up to and including the crucifixion are littered with king and kingdom language. The writers of the gospels wanted to show something particular about *this* King and *this* Kingdom.

Below are phrases from the descriptions of Holy Week in the gospels. Reflect on these words, perhaps underline phrases or doodle and draw in the margins. What does God reveal to you about his kingship and Kingdom through these texts?

> "...Pilate then went back inside the palace, summoned Jesus and asked him, 'Are you the king of the Jews?'" (John 18:33)

> "Jesus said: "My Kingdom is not of this world. If it were, my servants would fight to prevent my arrest by the Jewish leaders. But now my Kingdom is from another place.'" (John 18:36)

> "[The Roman soldiers] stripped him and put a scarlet robe on him, and then twisted together a crown of thorns and set it on his head. They put a staff in his right hand. Then they knelt in front of him and mocked him. 'Hail, king of the Jews!' they said." (Matt 27:28-29)

> "There was a written notice above him, which read: 'This is the King of the Jews.'" (Luke 23:38)

> "One of the criminals who hung there ... said: 'Jesus, remember me when you come into your Kingdom.' Jesus answered him, 'Truly I tell you, today you will be with me in paradise.'" (Luke 23:42-43)

Pray: What response do these passages stir in you? Bring your thoughts, prayers and worship to Jesus the King.

Holy Suspense

ADVENT 1

1.1 - AT THE SAME TIME

"In all this you greatly rejoice, though now for a little while you may have had to suffer grief in all kinds of trials." (1 Peter 1:6)

Read: 1 Peter 1:3-9

Every parent will know the scene. Your child has finally got completely absorbed in a book, Lego model or other activity *just* at the moment when it's time to make them stop and eat dinner. The typical conversation in our house at those times goes: "I know you want to keep playing / reading / watching, *but* the dinner is on the table." They ignore us. It escalates. Things get ugly.

A child psychologist, writing in a parenting book, encouraged us to make one simple change to the above encounter. "I know you want to keep playing / reading / watching, *and at the same time* the dinner is on the table."

Do you see it? The tiny change is to remove the word "but" and replace it with "and at the same time". Sounds too simple to make a difference, right? But we tried it. It works. It seems that the "but" is significant. It has the effect of negating everything that has gone before. So you give with one hand ("I know you want to keep playing...) and then immediately take away with the other ("but that doesn't matter now - what matters is we eat"). Unfortunately, Christians do "but" all the time:

> "You feel sick? *But* Jesus said he would always heal us if we have faith."
> "You're sad? *But* the Bible says be always joyful."
> "You want to help the poor? *But* Jesus said the poor would always be with us."
> "You're struggling with faith? *But* Paul says believe and don't doubt."

This attitude ignores the New Testament's posture of "at the same time", or what is sometimes called the "now and not yet" of God's Kingdom.

Just look at how masterfully Peter holds the tension in today's passage, inviting us to hold the future glory in tension with present suffering in our own lives:

"In his great mercy **he has given us** new birth	*in the past*
into a living **hope** through the resurrection of Jesus Christ from the dead, and into an **inheritance** that can never perish, spoil or fade. This **inheritance** is kept in heaven for you, who through faith are shielded by God's power until the **coming** of the salvation that is ready **to be revealed** in the **last time.**	*in the future*
In all this you greatly rejoice, though **now** for a little while you may have had to suffer grief in all kinds of trials." (1:3b-6)	*in the present*

Reflect: What is going on in the world around you, about which you need to say "at the same time"? Look at the examples below, and add some of your own:

God is our healer	*and at the same time*	**we won't all be healed this side of eternity.**
Jesus is our joy	*and at the same time*	**sadness is part of life before Jesus returns.**
	and at the same time	
	and at the same time	
	and at the same time	

Pray: Turn these statements into prayer, talking honestly to God about them and asking to know his presence in the middle of them.

1.2 - MARANATHA

"He who testifies to these things says, 'Yes, I am coming soon.'" (Revelation 22:20)

Read: 1 Corinthians 16:19-24

Sara comes from Sweden, and as a family we've discovered there are some words in Swedish with no direct English equivalent. So in our house we sometimes drop a Swedish word into conversation: *fika* (coffee, cake and chat); *lagom* (not too little or too much, just right); *mysa* (to have a cosy time with the lights low). Words like this are beyond functional - they reveal something about Swedish values and attitudes.

Paul's letters are mostly written in Greek, but when he closes 1 Corinthians he uses a surprise Aramaic word - *Maranatha*. This suggests that *Maranatha* was a common phrase of worship and prayer handed down from the earliest Aramaic speaking followers of Jesus, and that it had a particular importance and resonance for the ongoing church. Today we use ancient words like *Hallelujah, Hosanna* and *Amen* in a similar way - they have become part of the vocabulary of our worship.

So what does *Maranatha* mean? It is commonly translated "Come, Lord" (echoing Revelation 22:20), but Bible scholar Kenneth Bailey points out that there are really three possibilities:

"As often observed, this last word can be read *maran atha* (Our Lord has come). This translation addresses the readers and affirms a reality in the present (he is here). The two Aramaic words can also be divided to read *marana tha* (Our Lord-come!). This is a request addressed to the risen Lord that looks to the end of all things with the plea 'Please come!' A variant on this second option is, 'Our Lord is coming.' This also looks to the future but it is a statement of fact rather than a plea, and it is not addressed to Jesus." *Paul Through Mediterranean Eyes*, pages 495-496.

Bailey shows how all three translations have been adopted through church history, and that the version which is most unusual to us in the West, the past-tense confession "Our Lord has come" has in fact been the favoured interpretation in Middle Eastern countries.

In the spirit of "at the same time", we would like to suggest that *Maranatha* invites us to pray three things at once:

> Our Lord has come.
> Our Lord is coming.
> Our Lord - come!

This seems to us to be a helpful way of holding the tensions of Advent. We can declare with confidence that Jesus came in the incarnation. We can proclaim with hope that he is coming again. We can call to him in faith, interceding for our world and asking him to be present in our midst as we wait for his final return.

Pray: Make *Maranatha* your prayer today. You could make a list of prayer needs, or get creative with drawing, collaging or using digital photos to create a prayer board. Then over each person or situation, declare with faith the three-fold prayer above - that Jesus has come, is coming, and ask him to be present in those places.

1.3 - BE READY, BE WATCHFUL

"So you also must be ready, because the Son of Man will come at an hour when you do not expect him."
(Matthew 24:44)

Read: Luke 21:25-36

In our recent history we have experienced a world that was not "ready" for the Covid-19 pandemic. Nobody was prepared for a disease on this scale, or for the impact the lockdown would have on societies. And everyone was surprised by the scarcity of that most basic of human supplies: the toilet roll.

Except, in the Hargreaves' household, we sort-of were. Being recent subscribers to an environmentally-friendly toilet paper service, we had not yet got the hang of managing the deliveries. So, having many rolls stacked into every corner of our house already, we then sheepishly took delivery of another 48 rolls just as the lockdown began. It sounds like we were luxuriously sorted for the length of the months ahead, but it turned out that stockpiling toilet paper was not the preparation we all needed for the impact 2020 would have on our lives. Every new week brought fresh practical and emotional challenges that required tools of a different kind - none of us were really prepared.

Our passage today is one of a series where Jesus tells us to be prepared. Some of the UK government's snappy pandemic advice to "Be Alert!" sounds like an echo of Jesus' words here: "Be careful...", "Be always on the watch..." (v 34, 36). And our response to Jesus might be similar: "I'm tired of being alert! I don't even know quite what to watch out for!"

Some of our confusion comes from the fact that in Luke 21, Jesus is not only referring to his eventual second coming. He combines language about the Son of Man returning in great glory (v 27) with more imminent warnings to his generation about the destruction of the Jerusalem temple (look at 21:5-6, 20-24, 32). We know from the history books that the demolition of the temple by the Roman army really happened in 70 AD, and the eyewitness accounts sound just as dreadful as Jesus' descriptions in verse 20 and onwards.

We may not be 1st Century believers suffering the fall of Jerusalem, but we can relate to Jesus' warnings in verses 9-11 about wars, disasters and pestilences (aka pandemics). Living between Jesus' first and second comings is not promised to be a bed of roses. In 21:34-36 Jesus spells out what it means to be ready, awake and prepared. He knows how easily we get distracted, and he loves us so much that he doesn't want our hearts to be weighed down with the "anxieties of life" and whatever our drug of choice is - be it alcohol, Netflix or shopping.

There is hope in the midst of the disaster language: "When these things begin to take place, stand up and lift up your heads, because your redemption is drawing near" (v 28). No-one knows what the future will bring, or when Jesus will finally return. But as Jesus' followers we can anticipate the future with our eyes fixed on him.

Reflect: Think about what distracts you from watchfulness. Are there ways you can simplify your life to keep your heart in a healthy place? Are there practical things - getting enough sleep or exercise, a daily time for prayer, communication with a good friend, or something else that can help you live with freedom and peace?

Pray: Offer these things to God in prayer.

1.4 - READY OR NOT, HERE I COME...

"Therefore keep watch, because you do not know the day or the hour.." (Matthew 25:13)

Read: Matthew 25:1-13

Have you ever played hide-and-seek with toddlers? They're cute and funny, but useless at the game! When it's their turn to hide, more often than not they will be sniggering behind some leaf, or corner of a curtain, clearly visible to anyone with the slightest bit of eyesight. You call out "Ready or not - here I come!", and you can guarantee that in any true reading of the rules of hide-and-seek, the toddler will most definitely not be ready.

If Jesus called out "Ready or not - here I come!" - would we be like the toddlers in the game, woefully unprepared and not really even understanding the concept of preparation? Or would we be like the well-organised bridesmaids in Jesus' parable?

Just like the warnings from Jesus which we read yesterday, this passage is also about how to wait, but this time he makes the point using a story. Jesus, as always, uses everyday imagery for his parables. Everyone listening would have been to a village wedding, everyone would have known someone who consistently went out with too little oil and had to borrow from a friend. Perhaps you have friends who are forever forgetting their wallet, or family members who always forget to bring a water bottle, and you learn to expect their request for you to share. Except in this story, there's a chilling twist: no one has enough to share. If you didn't prepare, there will be no one to fall back on!

I once saw a joke stuck to the wall of a church office which said: "Jesus is coming... Look busy." Perhaps this is how we tend to read Jesus' parables and warnings about being ready. We have known enough overbearing parents, teachers and bosses to make us expect the same kind of un-grace from God. We expect him to be like the police officer just waiting to catch someone out.

But take a second look at Jesus' parable. Notice *what* it is that the bridesmaids are waiting for. They are not keeping their lamps lighted because a tyrannical boss told them to, nor is it much of a chore. The setting is a celebration, a community party, a time for joy and excitement.

Jesus is not telling us to keep watch just to keep us busy and out of trouble; he is wanting to make sure we don't miss out on the party! If I invite friends to a celebration, and then the morning of the event send them a message telling them to start early because a road accident has just been announced, no one would read my message and think me a kill-joy. They would understand that it came out of my desire for them to celebrate with me.

Jesus wants you to be ready for the day of the celebration, he doesn't want you to miss out.

Reflect: What kinds of things do you look forward to in the full coming of the Kingdom of God? Many Bible passages speak of God's coming Kingdom as a feast, a party, a celebration (Is 25:6-8; Rev 19:6-9. 21:1-4). What wonderful, joyful things can you imagine being part of God's renewed earth?

Pray: With that picture of eternity in your mind, how does it shape the idea of you being "ready"? How can you anticipate the delights of the Kingdom of God in your everyday life, work and play today?

1.5 - REFLECTING ON YOUR WEEK
"In the last days, God says, I will pour out my Spirit on all people." (Acts 2:17)

This week we've been thinking about living in the light of the coming of Jesus. Reflect on your life in this last week, using the timeline below. When did you feel hopeful? What felt hopeless or challenging? You can write, doodle or draw.

The past week   Today   Next week

Peter told the people in Acts 2 that in these "last days", God would pour out his Holy Spirit on us. Look forward to the week ahead: how does God want you to live? Ask for his Holy Spirit to empower you for that.

Active

Patience

ADVENT 2

2.1 - BEING STILL TO WAIT
"Be still before the Lord and wait patiently for him."
(Psalm 37:7)

Read: Psalm 37:1-7

We live in a fast-paced world, and often, around Advent, it only gets faster. In a typical year, school nativity plays, church events, shopping trips, parties and family gatherings absorb our attention, and any lulls in activity will probably find us on our phones and other devices, checking-in, uploading, watching, commenting... Repeat until collapse on Boxing Day.

After many years of this kind of rhythm, I am slowly waking up to a deeper truth. I have had to acknowledge that I am addicted to rush and hurry, feeling guilty unless I am juggling at least three tasks at any one time. Is that your experience too?

Reflect: In what ways does your life feel rushed, or your soul feel hurried?

John Mark Comer writes of mindset-shifting wisdom he received from his mentor: "I cannot live in the Kingdom of God with a hurried soul." (*The Ruthless Elimination of Hurry*, page 25). I have come to realise that all my rushing around might be a major block to growing with God; to becoming Christ-like.

In our passage for today the psalmist invites us to a different way of life, to be still and wait. Imagine that: you turn off the phone, put down the to-do list, choose not to be "productive" for a moment. How does that idea make you feel?

In the Bible, the alternative to hurry isn't to sit around being lazy. It is to take some intentional time to "sabbath" (which can be translated both "to stop" and "to delight"), whether that looks like a whole day, or an hour with the door closed, or five minutes of silence and stillness to just be with God. This means pro-actively planning, choosing, even diarising time to be still and wait on God.

The palmist writes some beautiful words which we could all do with meditating on:

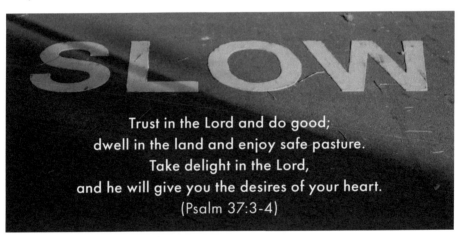

Trust in the Lord and do good;
dwell in the land and enjoy safe pasture.
Take delight in the Lord,
and he will give you the desires of your heart.
(Psalm 37:3-4)

We will only start to trust the Lord when we stop trusting in our own activity. When we pause to look around us we can be attentive to the places we dwell in. We will delight in the Lord when the other distractions are put in their place and God is our primary focus. As we choose to be still and wait on him, allowing our hearts to align with his, we will find the psalmist's words to be true: "... he will give you the desires of your heart."

Pray: Take a moment to begin this right now. Find a quiet place. Choose to acknowledge God's presence with you. When other thoughts come into your mind, notice them and then put them to one side. It may be just 2 minutes, or 10 minutes - this is not a competition or a chore. God just longs to be with you.

2.2 - THREE MILE AN HOUR GOD

"Come to me, all you who are weary and burdened, and I will give you rest." (Matthew 11:28)

Read: Luke 8:40-48

Yesterday we thought about our culture's addiction to hurry. We didn't touch on the truth that not everyone *can* hurry. Those of us who have disabilities, or are housebound, or who struggle with technology can be deeply frustrated by the slow pace of our lives. The 2020 lockdown gave most people an enforced time of pausing, causing both agitation and anxiety.

In the middle of this, God may be inviting us to choose how we respond when the brakes come on. Will we simply get annoyed? Or will we open ourselves up to the revelation of God's character that can come from an unhurried pace?

In Luke 8, Jesus is called to an emergency where a girl of around twelve is dying. Most of us would rush to help, but Jesus is characteristically unhurried. He takes the time to stop on the way and give attention to the woman who has been bleeding for twelve years. I love this line:

"Then the woman, *seeing that she could not go unnoticed...*" (Luke 8:47)

Because Jesus is unhurried, nobody can "go unnoticed". Her bleeding meant she was considered ceremonially unclean. If Jesus hadn't stopped she would not have been re-accepted back into religious society. Jesus' slow pace means he sees her, values her, and restores her both physically and into community.

Japanese theologian Kosuke Koyama called Jesus the "Three Mile an Hour God" because of his walking pace, explaining:

"God walks slowly because he is love. If he is not love he would have gone much faster. Love has its speed. It is an inner speed, it is a spiritual speed... It is the speed we walk and therefore it is the speed the love of God walks." *Three Mile an Hour God*, page 7.

Reflect: Bring to mind a situation where you were forced to slow down, or engage with someone who could not rush. Remember how it felt to go at an unhurried pace. Ask God to speak to you through that experience. What does it show you about yourself, God and the world around you?

Pray: Pause to pray through the following verse, asking God that you would be able to step into Jesus' invitation:

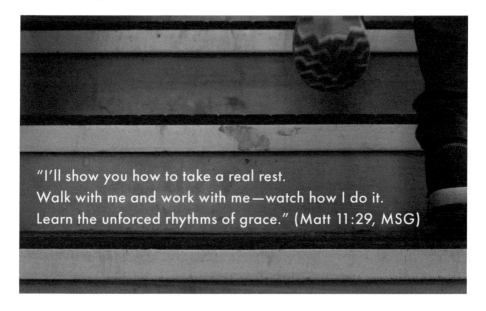

"I'll show you how to take a real rest.
Walk with me and work with me—watch how I do it.
Learn the unforced rhythms of grace." (Matt 11:29, MSG)

2.3 - WAITING AND GROANING

**"... we ourselves, who have the firstfruits of the Spirit, groan inwardly as we wait eagerly for our adoption."
(Romans 8:23)**

Read: Romans 8:18-27

Some waiting is just frustrating - impatience as a website loads slowly; irritation that the bus still hasn't come; annoyance at that friend who always shows-up twenty minutes late. But there are other things we wait for which move beyond frustration and into emotional pain or physical suffering. It could be the long-awaited return of a loved one, or anticipating an operation on a painful area of our body, or a longing for justice in an unfair situation.

Reflect: Are there things you have waited for in the past, or are anticipating now, which are difficult and painful?

Paul tells us that this is not unusual for the Christian. In fact, it is this painful state of waiting, "groaning as in the pains of childbirth" (8:22) in which the whole of creation has been engaged since the Fall. Paul declares that all creation - the very physical stuff of earth - will be renewed by God:

> "The creation itself will be liberated from its bondage to decay and brought into the freedom and glory of the children of God." (Romans 8:21)

In a similar way, for us humans, it is not just our souls and spirits that will be redeemed but our *bodies*, our whole selves (8:23). God's promise is to restore all that he has made. Right now, this remains not-yet a reality. It is "a sure and certain hope", but a hope for which we continue to wait, because "hope that is seen is no hope at all" (v 24).

In the meantime we groan as creation groans. Not "moaning": complaining and grumbling about minor troubles to anyone who will listen, but the lament of the Christian, full of the Spirit and aching to know God's Kingdom come in its fullness. Lament addresses our pain, our doubts, our frustrations and questions to God. In lament we pour out our hearts as "the Spirit himself intercedes for us through wordless groans" (v 26). We see that the earth is not how it is supposed to be, and join with Jesus as he weeps over a broken world (Luke 19:41).

It is vital that we voice these groans, mourning our losses and being honest before God. As Bible scholar Walter Brueggemann puts it:

> "Real prayer is being open about the negatives and yielding them to God... they are never yielded unless they be fully expressed." *The Message of the Psalms*, page 66.

Create: Your "groans" can look and sound a multitude of different ways - you might find it helpful to write them out, or shout at God, or sing your lament, or create art or collage to express your heart. They can be as simple as a whispered, honest prayer or as complex as Górecki's *Symphony of Sorrowful Songs* (a moving piece of music to listen to while you lament). The important thing is that we express these things to God.

Pray: Take some time to voice your groans to God today. Know that he listens, and he responds.

2.4 - THE SLOW WORK OF GOD

"You know that under pressure, your faith-life is forced into the open and shows its true colours. So don't try to get out of anything prematurely."
(James 1:2-4, MSG)

Take some time to reflect on this wisdom from Jesuit priest Teilhard de Chardin.

Above all, trust in the slow work of God.
We are quite naturally impatient in everything
to reach the end without delay.
We should like to skip the intermediate stages.
We are impatient of being on the way to something unknown,
something new.

And yet it is the law of all progress
that it is made by passing through some stages of instability—
and that it may take a very long time.

And so I think it is with you;
your ideas mature gradually—let them grow,
let them shape themselves, without undue haste.
Don't try to force them on,
as though you could be today what time
(that is to say, grace and circumstances acting on your own good will)
will make of you tomorrow.

Only God could say what this new spirit
gradually forming within you will be.
Give Our Lord the benefit of believing
that his hand is leading you,
and accept the anxiety of feeling yourself
in suspense and incomplete.

Pierre Teilhard de Chardin, SJ. Taken from *Hearts on Fire: Praying with the Jesuits*, edited by Michael Harter, page 102.

Reflect: How might these words apply to your life? What "intermediate stages" are you keen to skip? What examples of the "law of all progress" can you think of in nature? What would it look like to "accept the anxiety of feeling yourself in suspense and incomplete"?

Pray: Talk to God about how you feel. Ask him to help you trust in his slow work in your life. You may find it helpful to picture God as your perfect gardener, or artist, or mentor, who allows you to grow and develop slowly, with care but without controlling you. Know that he sees your full potential and is patiently delighting as that unfolds in you, day by day.

Advent:
**unseen bulbs asleep in frozen earth.
Handwritten markers
hold promises
of spring colours.**

#TinyAdventPoems 13/24
Text - Amy Scott Robinson | Design - Richard Lyall

2.5 - SIMPLIFYING PRAYER

"Return to your rest, my soul, for the Lord has been good to you." (Psalm 116:7)

Read: Psalm 116:1-7

Psalm 116 tells of a God who is full of compassion towards us, always hearing our prayers and actively responding with grace and justice. At the same time, he is also the God who brings peace and rest. Sometimes it can help to use fewer words when we pray, approaching God less like a slot-machine and more as our friend who loves to spend time in our presence.

The following idea is a commonly used exercise using Psalm 46:10, helping us to simplify our thoughts and relax in God's presence. Find a quiet place (or put on some quiet, instrumental music) and make yourself comfortable. Take a moment to slow your breathing, and decide to spend this time just being still before God, with no other agenda.

Speak out the first line of the prayer, and then hold it in your mind as you take a few more deep breaths. Then speak the next, shorter line, and repeat the process. After the final "Be", just relax in God's presence for as long as you feel comfortable.

Be still and know that I am God.

Be still and know that I Am.

Be still and know.

Be still.

Be.

Hope-filled Expectation

ADVENT 3

3.1 - GRIEVING WITH HOPE

"... do not grieve like the rest of humankind, who have no hope." (1 Thessalonians 4:13)

Read: 1 Thessalonians 4:13-18

Last week we thought about "groaning" with creation - expressing our struggles to God in honesty and lament. Related to this is the subject of grieving. Henri Nouwen writes:

> "There are so few mourners left in this world. But grief is the discipline of the heart that sees the sin of the world, and knows itself to be the sorrowful price of freedom without which love cannot bloom. I am beginning to see that much of praying is grieving." *The Return of the Prodigal Son*, page 129.

Jesus shows us how to grieve and love and pray. He wept with Mary and Martha at Lazarus' tomb, before calling out in prayer to his loving Father (John 11). He taught "Blessed are those who mourn" (Matt 5:4), echoing the psalmist's statement that "The Lord is close to the broken-hearted and saves those who are crushed in spirit." (Ps 34:18)

Has that been your experience? Do you feel God's presence extra close in times of grief? Many of us may have been taught that Christians ought to always be joyful, and we may not even dare to bring our grief before God, missing out on the promised blessing of his comfort and presence.

We see in Jesus that grief is acceptable,

and that we should mourn. But Paul makes an important distinction in today's passage: we do not grieve "like the rest of humankind, who have no hope". He goes on to remind us that as Jesus was resurrected from the dead, all who die "in Jesus" will also be resurrected. This will happen on the day when Jesus returns, his "second coming".

This passage from Thessalonians uses a lot of picture language, and has often been mis-read as being about some sort of "rapture" up to heaven. Instead we need to understand the ancient imagery of a king returning to his home city. The people would go out to meet their ruler as he approached the city - so we are pictured meeting Jesus as he comes down (v 17).

Our hope is not in our removal from the planet we call home. The point Paul is making is that death, although tragic and worth grieving, does not have the final word. We have a hope beyond our current circumstances, a hope of life with Jesus for eternity on a renewed earth (see Revelation 21:1-5).

It's another beautiful tension for our Christian life: Yes, it is right that we mourn with stark honesty before God, and at the same time we hold on to the promise of our eternal hope. And, we must, as verse 18 states: "...encourage each other with these words."

Pray: What do you mourn in the world or in your life right now? Be completely honest with God about it.

Activity: Is there anyone in your Christian community who needs to be encouraged with words reminding them of their eternal hope in Christ? Perhaps take a moment to write a card or a quick text message, or give them a call.

3.2 - JESUS GRIEVES FOR JOHN THE BAPTIST

"When Jesus heard what had happened, he withdrew by boat privately to a solitary place." (Matthew 14:13)

Read: Matthew 11:2-6 and 14:1-13

The third week in Advent invites us to spend time in the story of John the Baptist. Although honoured by Jesus as "the greatest among those born of women" (11:11), his story is also one of vulnerability and grief.

We see John's doubts openly expressed in chapter 11: languishing in prison, he wonders if Jesus really is the one he had thought him to be. We may hope that the message back from Jesus about the signs of the Kingdom would have brought John hope and joy, but the text doesn't tell us this. We only know of the sad ending of John's life as retold in chapter 14. In verse 13 we are told how Jesus responds to this awful event: the horrific murder of his cousin.

In the world all around us, we see the consequences of a broken humanity coping poorly with grief and sadness. There are those who bottle it up until it spills over into domestic abuse, those who try to forget by misusing alcohol or other substances and others who, in a more socially acceptable way, bury themselves in work to the detriment of both stress levels and family life. As Christians we may fall into the trap of singing our joyful songs louder.

Reflect: How do you respond to overwhelming emotions? Do you have coping mechanisms for when the wave of grief knocks you sideways?

Jesus' response to grief is to take time out. We know from Luke 5:16 that "Jesus often withdrew to lonely places and prayed." The nature of the "lonely place" is that no one was near to take note of how Jesus prayed, what words he used. But we know that he was honest with his Father, and he models for us how to do the same. It is important to note that Jesus knew about eternal hope, he understood the important role John had played in God's Kingdom plan (11:12-14), and yet he had an emotional response of grief at news of his friend's death. Worshipping in the waiting involves cries of lament in the same breath as proclamations of the sure hope we have in Christ.

Today, you may find it helpful to listen to Sam's song "There's a Time For Tears", and spend a moment expressing emotions of grief and loss before your God who listens. **engageworship.org/tears**

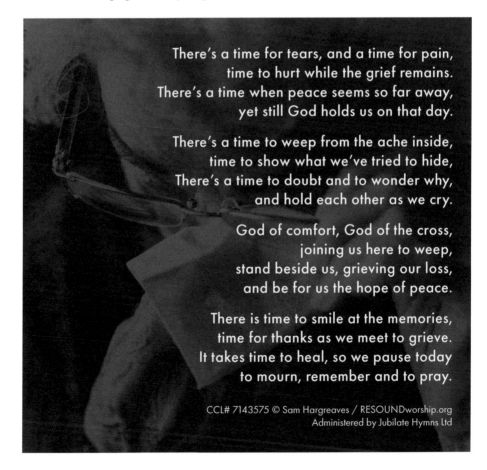

There's a time for tears, and a time for pain,
time to hurt while the grief remains.
There's a time when peace seems so far away,
yet still God holds us on that day.

There's a time to weep from the ache inside,
time to show what we've tried to hide,
There's a time to doubt and to wonder why,
and hold each other as we cry.

God of comfort, God of the cross,
joining us here to weep,
stand beside us, grieving our loss,
and be for us the hope of peace.

There is time to smile at the memories,
time for thanks as we meet to grieve.
It takes time to heal, so we pause today
to mourn, remember and to pray.

CCL# 7143575 © Sam Hargreaves / RESOUNDworship.org
Administered by Jubilate Hymns Ltd

3.3 - INVESTING IN THE AGE TO COME
"...godliness with contentment is great gain."
(1 Timothy 6:6)

Read: 1 Timothy 6:6-19

What kind of Christmas spender are you? Are you the budgeting type, who has a spreadsheet each year, weighing up the cost of food while also keeping each child's gift list balanced? Or perhaps you are the spontaneous type who only realises on Christmas morning quite how many gifts you've bought for your loved ones, and then lives on baked beans throughout January?

It is not easy to withstand the temptations all around us around this time of year, especially the Christmas adverts that seem to say "if you love someone, buy them this." By the New Year, many of us look at the debris of toys and trinkets and realise we have been steered by "foolish and harmful desires", as Paul puts it in verse 9.

It would be a mistake to think of Paul as the spartan, joyless type, however. He confesses to faith in a God who "...richly provides us with everything for our enjoyment" (v 17). Did you catch that last word? "Enjoyment"! God wants us to enjoy the good things of creation.

The risk, in Paul's mind, is when the "stuff" rates higher than God: when we spend more time on our relationship with money and things than on our relationship with God. For every gadget we buy, we need to spend time to care for it and money updating it; the larger the house, the more time spent on household chores; the bigger the trust funds, the bigger the headaches in how to invest.

God longs that we put our hope in him, because he is trustworthy, rather than in wealth which "is so uncertain" (v 17). Paul encourages those with money to spare (and if you are reading this from a paper book or on a device in the Western world, count yourself in) to invest in a different kind of bank account. This investment scheme builds up true treasure, providing a firm foundation for the age to come (v 19).

Paul promises not just fantastic returns on this investment, but also the gift of "life that is truly life". How do we deposit into this high-interest scheme? It's a three-point process: 1) Do good and be rich in good deeds, 2) be generous and 3) be willing to share (v 18).

If these words feel uncomfortable to you, and you feel resistance in your heart; don't start in verse 18 of this passage. Much better to start at the beginning, in verse 6. Because when we find that we are actually content, sharing is no trouble at all.

Reflect: Where are you on the scale of contentment in life? How could you grow in gratitude for what you have, and in godly generosity?

Pray: Bring these reflections honestly to God. Remember that he is not meeting you as a judge with a big stick, but rather as a loving parent, longing for you to make space for him in your life. Ask God if there is "stuff" that is taking up the time and space that should be occupied by him. Ask God to help you simplify your life by investing in the age to come.

3.4 - A CONTENTED CHILD
"I have calmed and quietened myself."
(Psalm 131:2)

There are few things more beautiful than a child asleep (although those who agree with this statement may do so based on their experience of a tired child, not asleep). When the anxious fretting, or violent outbursts, or inconsolable weeping finally ends and the child is fast asleep, the peace and the relief is palpable. A child, sleeping safely in a parent's arms, is fully relaxed, at a level that adults rarely reach. This child is the image of trust; it's truly non-anxious, unrushed and contented.

Spend some time with Psalm 131. Doodle and scribble around this page, reflecting on how the words speak to you. To what level can you say these words along with the psalmist? Are there parts that encourage you or challenge you? What would total contentment and trust in God look like to you?

Allow your doodles and questions to turn into prayers to God, whatever those need to be.

God, I'm not trying to rule the roost,
I don't want to be king of the mountain.
I haven't meddled where I have no business
or fantasized grandiose plans.

I've kept my feet on the ground,
I've cultivated a quiet heart.
Like a baby content in its mother's arms,
my soul is a baby content.

Wait, Israel, for God. Wait with hope.
Hope now; hope always!

(Psalm 131:1-3, MSG)

3.5 - THE WAITING FATHER

Read: Luke 15:11-31

Reflect, write, draw or doodle around the image below as you consider this question: what does it mean that God is the Father who waits?

Awe-struck Anticipation

ADVENT 4

Note: these reflections
are not numbered.
Read Christmas Day on
the day it falls, and the
others as works for you.

CHRISTMAS DAY

Read: Luke 2:1-20

Early one Christmas morning, arms laden with gifts, food and drinks, our friend Charis rang the doorbell of her brother's house. It was answered by her nephew, a small boy, wide-eyed and overflowing with excitement: "He's here! Jesus has come!"

It turned out that, during Advent, the family had been slowly building their nativity set, piece by piece, day by day. They started with Mary, then added Angel Gabriel, Joseph, shepherds and assorted animals, as well as furniture including an empty manger. By the time they reached Christmas Eve, only one character had not yet appeared. The young boy had gone to bed that night with all anticipation of gifts, parties, and food secondary to a single, vital question: Would Jesus arrive on Christmas Day?

This is the true waiting of Advent, the true gift of Christmas. It is the song of Isaiah from hundreds of years previous: "The virgin will conceive and give birth to a son, and will call him Immanuel." (7:14)

Immanuel - God with us. He's here!

It's the joy of the Angels on the hillside, announcing to the shepherds:

"Do not be afraid. I bring you good news that will cause great joy for all the people. Today in the town of David a Saviour has been born to you; he is the Messiah, the Lord. This will be a sign to you: you will find a baby wrapped in cloths and lying in a manger." (Luke 2:10-12)

The Messiah - the promised one. *Yeshua* - the saviour. He's here!

This is the deeper truth rung out by chapel bells and carolling choirs. It's the root of our gift-giving and our family celebrations. It's what every Scrooge and Grinch hungers for most fundamentally in their cold heart - the knowledge that they are loved, known and befriended by the creator of the universe, the Word made flesh, God with us.

Pray: Wherever you are, whatever is going on today, you are not alone. Pause to receive this gift for yourself today: Jesus has come. God is with you.

THE WAITING LISTS
"May your word to me be fulfilled." (Luke 1:38)

Read: Matthew 1:1-17

When I open Matthew's gospel to read his Christmas account, I'm tempted to skip the first seventeen verses. That list of names doesn't really strike me as an inspiring, page-turning read. But if we pause and reflect for a moment we may discover that God has something to say to us.

Firstly, we can think of these genealogies as "waiting lists". Matthew's list begins with Abraham, who waited (not always patiently) for his promised heir, and looked forward to descendants as numerous as the stars in the sky (Gen 15:5). He never saw the fullness of this promise, but he waited with faith, believing that one day God would fulfil his covenant. Reading Matthew's list we continue to meet people who lived by faith in God (so Hebrews 11 tells us) awaiting God's answers which they did not see fulfilled in their lifetime.

> "These were all commended for their faith, yet none of them received what had been promised, since God had planned something better for us so that only together with us would they be made perfect." (Hebrews 11:39-40)

These lists remind us that the coming of Jesus was the fulfilment of hundreds of years of waiting. This is the culmination of all the covenants, prophesies and promises. It is the crux of the whole grand story of God's interaction with humanity, funnelled down into the most humble, unlikely setting possible.

As CS Lewis put it:

> "The whole thing narrows and narrows, until at last it comes down to a little point, small as the point of a spear - a Jewish girl at her prayers." *God in the Dock*, page 84.

This leads us on to the second thing about Matthew's list. Genealogies of that time would have only included men, but Matthew breaks with convention by including four women. If their sex wasn't scandalous enough, consider the fact that some of them were also gentiles, and most of them were of dubious reputation. Yet Kenneth Bailey points out that in their stories "all four women demonstrate intelligence, boldness and courage." He concludes:

> "With such a list Matthew gives us clues about the kinds of people that the Messiah came to save. He was to be a Saviour for women and men who were both saints and sinners, Jews and Gentiles." *Jesus Through Middle Eastern Eyes*, page 42.

Reflect: Jesus came to save all kinds of people, even those rejected by society. Are there people you can show Jesus' love and acceptance to?

The list lands on a fifth woman - Mary. She was young, female, and as yet unmarried. Her pregnancy would most likely cause her shame in the community, and yet she continues in the line of Tamar, Rahab, Ruth and Bathsheba by playing her part with courage and trust. She responds to God: "May your word to me be fulfilled" (Luke 1:38).

Pray: Is God calling you to something, to which you can respond with the courage and trust of Mary? Bring these reflections to God in prayer.

A NEPALESE CAROL
"See the vision of the newborn Lord."

Read: Matthew 2:1-18

People celebrate Christmas all over the world, with all kinds of traditions and songs. Stepping outside of what is familiar to us can help us see Christmas through fresh eyes.

We love the beautiful recording of *Herana*, a traditional Nepalese carol by the band Aradhna (you can listen to it here - **engageworship.org/aradhna**). Singer Chris Hale has written:

> "I grew up in Nepal, singing this song every year on what was called *Bara Din* (the Great Day), every December 25th. It was against the law to become a devotee of Jesus (*Yeshu*) in Nepal at that time, and one could be put in prison for a year for doing so. We often used to meet with other devotees in secret. But we always sang. There was so much joy. No one seemed afraid." (Liner notes from the album "Namaste Saté".)

This translation of the lyrics helps us understand why this story brought joy and comfort to a persecuted group of believers.

> Look up into the sky at the brightness of this star.
> Do not delay but come and see the vision of the newborn Lord.

> The Lord came to this world to fulfil the word of God,
> to understand the suffering of humanity he lay helpless in a manger.
> The shepherds stared in wonder at the angels.

Encouraged, they went on their way happily, telling the news.

The star cast its own light guiding astrologer kings.
Presenting gifts, they received a vision of the Lord .
Hearts full of joy, the Rescuer of a people lost in sin, is born!
Think not to the thorns in your feet.
Think not to the journey.
We move and breathe in him.

It may help you to put on this song, or just read through the lyrics and reflect on the saviour who "to understand the suffering of humanity lay helpless in a manger." Who revealed himself to poor shepherds and gentile magi. Who had to flee for his life from religious and political persecution of Herod which left countless mothers weeping (2:16-18). Who lifts our eyes from the thorns in our feet and invites us to move and breathe in him.

You may also want to put on this YouTube video of a Nepalese church, singing the same song with joy and celebration. **engageworship.org/herana**

Pray: For Nepal and other countries where Christians are persecuted, where Advent waiting may be more urgent and painful than ours. Give thanks for the hope of Christmas that has spread to every nation on the earth.

SIMEON AND ANNA

"She never left the temple but worshipped night and day, fasting and praying." (Luke 2:37)

Read: Luke 2:22-40

I wonder how you would feel if God gave you a particular task, a calling, and then asked you to wait eighty years before you could fulfil it? Would we consider our lives a waste, or meaningless? It certainly would fly in the face of our cultural ideals of youth. In a society where television newsreaders lose their jobs at the sight of their first wrinkle and silicon valley whizz kids make their first million before they're 21, the world doesn't consider age an asset any more.

And yet, Laura Ingalls Wilder published the first of her *Little House* books aged 65, Harold ("Colonel") Sanders was 62 when he franchised KFC and Nelson Mandela was 76 by the time he became prime minister of South Africa. And in the run up to his 100th birthday, Captain Sir Thomas Moore became a national hero in the UK, raising over £30 million for charity by walking laps of his garden.

In today's passage, we encounter a woman and a man who knew about long-term waiting. We don't know how long Simeon had waited for the fulfilment of God's promise that he would see the Messiah (2:26), but he is clearly not long for this world. Anna, we're told, has been a widow for 84 years. She has dedicated her whole life to worshipping, fasting and praying (2:37), and lived in expectancy of God's coming.

Imagine the scene as the Holy Spirit stirs them separately with the knowledge that this is it. This is the moment they've been waiting for. Not a lean-back-in-the-sofa kind of waiting. But an active anticipation, lives lived in prayerful and watchful expectation.

> "Sovereign Lord, as you have promised,
> you may now dismiss your servant in peace.
> For my eyes have seen your salvation,
> which you have prepared in the sight of all nations:
> a light for revelation to the Gentiles,
> and the glory of your people Israel." (Luke 2:29-32)

We would all hope to have that attitude towards the end of our lives: "...you may now dismiss your servant in peace." To know that our calling had been fulfilled, to be greeted as a "good and faithful servant" by the Master as in the parable of the talents (Matt 25:14-30).

Reflect: Spend some time reflecting on your own attitude to waiting and time. If God gave you a task, would you have a maximum amount of time that you would be prepared to wait? If you have dreams and hopes yet unfulfilled, would you have the patience to wait until you are near the end of your life to see them come to pass? Do you look at the older people in your life, perhaps family members or friends in church, with a low expectation of what God might do through them? Do you have low expectations of what God might be able to do through you as you age?

Pray: Make a list of older people in your life and pray that God might use them for his glory. Perhaps ask God for an encouraging word or Bible verse for them and write them a card.

JESUS GREW

"And Jesus grew in wisdom and stature, and in favour with God and people." (Luke 2:52)

Read: Luke 2:39-52

Waiting is for life, not just for Advent! We hope that the theme of this series has been life-giving and encouraging for you. In this last reflection we're going to think about how we take these principles into the year to come.

Have you ever thought about how much Jesus waited? The majority of the gospel stories cover Jesus' life when he was around 30-33 years of age. This means that for around 90% of his earthly existence he wasn't active in the ministry he was sent to fulfil. What would it have been like for Jesus, looking ahead and anticipating when his time would come? Was he impatient, frustrated, raring to go?

The end of Luke 2 gives us a snapshot of one story from this waiting phase. It seems that Jesus spent these first thirty years growing, letting his body develop physically and allowing God to fill him with wisdom and grace (v. 40). The eternal Son of God emptied himself in becoming a human being, which meant that he had to grow and develop in the same way we all do. It was a slow, gradual process, not the instant "zap" of maturity which we all think we would prefer!

In this passage we also read about him "lost" to his parents (a fairly typical situation in many families). They find him in the temple, listening to the teachers and asking questions. He chooses to be in a place where he can grow in his understanding about God. We're told that everyone is amazed by his understanding, and that he then goes home to continue growing "in wisdom and stature, and in favour with God and people" (v 52).

By joining us in the human process of maturing, Jesus relates to our experiences of developing slowly over time. Jesus responds to this period of waiting by putting himself in places where he can learn. Like Jesus, we can gain godly wisdom and understanding by listening and asking questions. We can use times of waiting to grow in our relationship with God and with the people around us. Patient, active waiting can develop us into the fullness of who God made us to be.

Reflect: As you look back at the year that has past, how can you see that God has grown and developed you?

As you think about this series on *Worship in the Waiting*, what have you discovered about God and yourself?

As you look forward to the year ahead, what are you waiting for? Where will you need God's patience? How would you like to grow in wisdom, understanding, relationships and the grace of God?

Pray: Commit yourself and your coming year to God.

Worship
IN THE
Waiting

An Advent journey of anticipation and expectation.

Prepare your heart and life for the coming King, exploring what it means to wait with active patience.

Bible reflections are paired with questions, creative responses and suggestions for practical application.

This resource is designed to work alongside the *Worship in the Waiting: Church Service Pack*.

Your *Personal Devotions* book also stands alone if you simply wish to read it by yourself. You could also adapt these reflections and activities for group discussion.

Sara and Sam Hargreaves run **engage**worship, producing creative resources for local churches. They both trained at London School of Theology and King's College London. This book is part of a series which also includes *Worship in the Wilderness* and *Harvest Worship*.

ISBN 978-1-83823-120-0

9 781838 231200

Published by

Music and Worship
Foundation

Printed on FSC certified paper

engage
worship